GEO

Lexile: _____
AR/BL: _____1.8_____
AR Points: ___0.5___

Comma

Mary Elizabeth Salzmann

Published by SandCastle™, an imprint of ABDO Publishing Company, 4940 Viking Drive, Edina, Minnesota 55435.

Printed in the United States.

Photo credits: PhotoDisc, Photosphere

Library of Congress Cataloging-in-Publication Data

Salzmann, Mary Elizabeth, 1968-
    Comma / Mary Elizabeth Salzmann.
        p. cm. -- (Punctuation)
    Includes index.
    ISBN 1-57765-620-2
    1. English language--Punctuation--Juvenile literature. 2. Comma--Juvenile literature.
    [1. English language--Punctuation. 2. Comma.] I. Title.

PE1450 .S24 2001
428.2--dc21

                                                                          2001022897

The SandCastle concept, content, and reading method have been reviewed and approved by a national advisory board including literacy specialists, librarians, elementary school teachers, early childhood education professionals, and parents.

Let Us Know

After reading the book, SandCastle would like you to tell us your stories about reading. What is your favorite page? Was there something hard that you needed help with? Share the ups and downs of learning to read. We want to hear from you! To get posted on the ABDO Publishing Company Web site, send us email at:

sandcastle@abdopub.com

About SandCastle™
Nonfiction books for the beginning reader

- Basic concepts of phonics are incorporated with integrated language methods of reading instruction. Most words are short, and phrases, letter sounds, and word sounds are repeated.

- Readability is determined by the number of words in each sentence, the number of characters in each word, and word lists based on curriculum frameworks.

- Full-color photography reinforces word meanings and concepts.

- "Words I Can Read" list at the end of each book teaches basic elements of grammar, helps the reader recognize the words in the text, and builds vocabulary.

- Reading levels are indicated by the number of flags on the castle.

Look for more SandCastle books in these three reading levels:

Level 1 (one flag)	**Level 2** (two flags)	**Level 3** (three flags)

Grades Pre-K to K 5 or fewer words per page	**Grades K to 1** 5 to 10 words per page	**Grades 1 to 2** 10 to 15 words per page

This is a **comma**.

I know when to use **commas**.

A **comma** shows where to pause in a sentence.

Jerome is reading, not watching TV.

If Luis blows too big a
bubble, it will pop.

Dave has a blue jacket and yellow binoculars, and Amy has a green thermos.

Commas go between things in a list.

Carl has goggles, a cape, and flippers.

Use a **comma** between two words that describe something.

Vicky has a soft, cuddly puppy.

Use a **comma** between a city and a state.

Mary is skiing in Vail, Colorado.

Use **commas** in dates.

Faith knows that the first Independence Day was July 4, 1776.

What are Elaine, Helen, and Tracy playing on?

(swings)

Words I Can Read

Nouns

A noun is a person, place, or thing

binoculars (buh-NOK-yuh-lurz) p. 11
bubble (BUH-buhl) p. 9
cape (KAPE) p. 13
city (SIT-ee) p. 17
comma (KOM-uh) pp. 5, 7, 15, 17

commas (KOM-uhz) pp. 5, 13, 19
dates (DAYTSS) p. 19
flippers (FLIP-urz) p. 13
goggles (GOG-uhlz) p. 13
jacket (JAK-it) p. 11
list (LIST) p. 13
puppy (PUHP-ee) p. 15

sentence (SEN-tuhnss) p. 7
state (STATE) p. 17
swings (SWINGZ) p. 21
thermos (THUR-muhss) p. 11
things (THINGZ) p. 13
TV (tee-VEE) p. 7
words (WURDZ) p. 15

Proper Nouns

A proper noun is the name of a person, place, or thing

Amy (AY-mee) p. 11
Carl (KARL) p. 13
Colorado (kol-ur-AD-oh) p. 17
Dave (DAYV) p. 11
Elaine (el-AYN) p. 21

Faith (FAYTH) p. 19
Helen (HEL-uhn) p. 21
Independence Day (in-di-PEN-duhnss DAY) p. 19
Jerome (je-ROME) p. 7

July (juh-LYE) p. 19
Luis (loo-EESS) p. 9
Mary (MAIR-ee) p. 17
Tracy (TRAY-see) p. 21
Vail (VAYL) p. 17
Vicky (VIK-ee) p. 15

Pronouns

A pronoun is a word that replaces a noun

I (EYE) p. 5
it (IT) p. 9

something (SUHM-thing) p. 15

this (THISS) p. 5
what (WUHT) p. 21

22

Verbs

A verb is an action or being word

are (AR) p. 21
blows (BLOHZ) p. 9
describe (di-SKRIBE) p. 15
go (GOH) p. 13
has (HAZ) pp. 11, 13, 15
know (NOH) p. 5

knows (NOHZ) p. 19
is (IZ) pp. 5, 7, 17
pause (PAWZ) p. 7
playing (PLAY-ing) p. 21
pop (POP) p. 9
reading (REED-ing) p. 7

shows (SHOHZ) p. 7
skiing (SKEE-ing) p. 17
use (YOOZ) pp. 5, 15, 17, 19
was (WUHZ) p. 19
watching (WOCH-ing) p. 7
will (WIL) p. 9

Adjectives

An adjective describes something

big (BIG) p. 9
blue (BLOO) p. 11
cuddly (KUDH-uhl-ee)
    p. 15

first (FURST) p. 19
green (GREEN) p. 11
soft (SAWFT) p. 15

two (TOO) p. 15
yellow (YEL-oh) p. 11

Adverbs

An adverb tells how, when, or where something happens

too (TOO) p. 9

Glossary

binoculars – something you look through with both eyes to make things that are far away seem closer

cape – a sleeveless coat that you tie around your neck and wear over your shoulders

flippers – long, flat rubber shoes that help you swim faster

goggles – large glasses that fit tightly over your eyes to protect them

jacket – a light coat you wear in the spring or fall

thermos – a container that keeps liquids hot or cold for a long time